TRIVIA
&
PUZZLE
FUN BOOK

TRIVIA & PUZZLE FUN BOOK

Kara Adamo

illustrated by Nancy Didion

SCHOLASTIC INC.
New York Toronto London Auckland Sydney

With thanks to Linda Lannon,
who told me to go for it

No part of this publication may be reproduced in whole or in part, or stored in a retrieval system, or transmitted in any form or by any means, electronic, mechanical, photocopying, recording, or otherwise, without written permission of the publisher. For information regarding permission, write to Scholastic Inc., 730 Broadway, New York, NY 10003.

ISBN 0-590-46065-X

12 11 10 9 8 7 6 5 4 3 2 1   2 3 4 5 6 7/9

Printed in the U.S.A.   40

First Scholastic printing, September 1992

TRIVIA
&
PUZZLE
FUN BOOK

INTRODUCTION

One day Kristy had a great idea. Wouldn't it be easy if a parent who needed a baby-sitter could call one number and reach four experienced baby-sitters at once That was a long time ago, and since then Kristy, Claudia, Mary Anne, and Stacey have welcomed alternate officer Dawn Schafer, junior officers Mallory Pike and Jessica Ramsey, and associate members Logan Bruno and Shannon Kilbourne into their club. But that's only the beginning of the adventures of the kids in the BSC. How much do you know about their adventures? How well do you really know the kids in the club?

Now you can quiz yourself and your friends on all of the fun facts about *The Baby-sitters Club*. So sharpen your pencil and turn the page because the BSC is waiting!

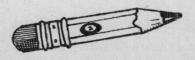

Wordsearch
THE CLUB

There are three parts to this puzzle which contains questions about the club itself.

First answer the trivia questions.

1. On what days of the week does the Baby-sitters Club meet? Monday, _Wednesday_ , and _Friday_ .

2. Kristy thought of the Baby-sitters Club when she noticed her mother having trouble finding a sitter for _____ .

3. Only two club members like to write in the Baby-sitters Club notebook. Who are they? Kristy and _____

4. What day of the week is dues day? _____

5. Kristy came up with this idea for a box that contains games and activities for baby-sitting charges. What is it called? _____

6. The Baby-sitters Club's brief competition was formed by Liz Lewis and was called:
The Baby-sitters _____

7. What time do the meetings begin? (spell it out)
_____ -thirty

8. How many times a week are the club members responsible for reading the entries in the Baby-sitters Club notebook? _____

9. This BSC member sits in a director's chair at the club meetings. _____

10. Club meetings are held in this member's bedroom. _____

Now find your answers in this word search puzzle. They are hidden horizontally, diagonally, vertically, and backward.

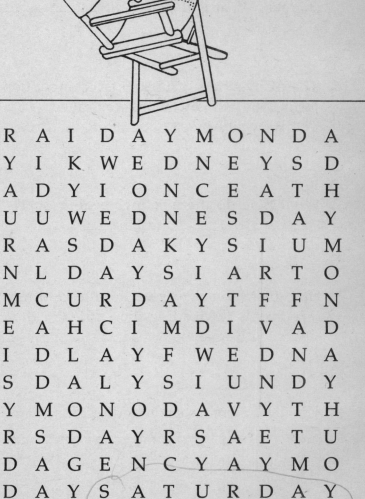

```
F  R  A  I  D  A  Y  M  O  N  D  A
K  Y  I  K  W  E  D  N  E  Y  S  D
R  A  D  Y  I  O  N  C  E  A  T  H
I  U  U  W  E  D  N  E  S  D  A  Y
S  R  A  S  D  A  K  Y  S  I  U  M
T  N  L  D  A  Y  S  I  A  R  T  O
Y  M  C  U  R  D  A  Y  T  F  F  N
L  E  A  H  C  I  M  D  I  V  A  D
R  I  D  L  A  Y  F  W  E  D  N  A
E  S  D  A  L  Y  S  I  U  N  D  Y
A  Y  M  O  N  O  D  A  V  Y  T  H
U  R  S  D  A  Y  R  S  A  E  T  U
R  D  A  G  E  N  C  Y  A  Y  M  O
N  D  A  Y  S  A  T  U  R  D  A  Y
```

When you've circled all the words in the puzzle, the remaining letters will spell out—from left to right—all the days of the week except one. That day is the answer to the SUPER TRIVIA QUESTION.

Example:

```
T  U  G  E  S  D  A  Y  W  E
D  N  R  E  K  I  D  K  I  T
S  D  E  A  Y  D  T  H  U  R
C  H  A  R  G  E  S  S  D  A
Y  F  T  R  I  A  D  A  Y  S
A  T  U  R  D  A  Y  S  U  N
D  A  Y  T  U  E  S  D  A  Y
```

TUESDAY,
WEDNESDAY,
THURSDAY,
FRIDAY,
SATURDAY,
SUNDAY,
TUESDAY

Answer: MONDAY

SUPER TRIVIA QUESTION

On what day of the week did Kristy get the idea for the Baby-sitters Club?

Maday

Backwords Scramble

#1

The answer is: BLASTO-PLANE, but what is the
question? Unscramble the letters in the words
below to solve this puzzle.

HTAW IS HTE

EMAN FO EHT YTO THTA

SI KTUSC NI AJKCEI YSDOROWKS

ORHABTOM NIRDA?

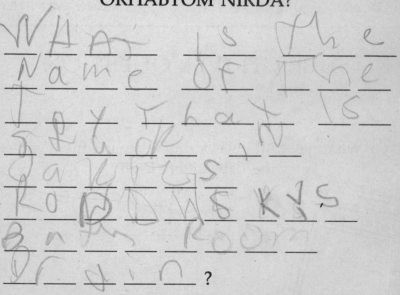

Picture Puzzle #1

To solve this puzzle, write the name of each picture in the blanks below. Cross out or add the indicated letters as you go along.

Example: ☆ − AR ÷ 1 + Y ÷ 🐦 − ID ÷ 🚪 − B

S T̶A̶R̶O N E Y B I R̶D̶ B O O K

Answer: STONEYBROOK

Which charge did Dawn help make a costume for Halloween?

JACKIE
_ _ _ _ _ _ _

RODOWSKY
_ _ _ _ _ _ _ _ _

What kind of costume did they make?

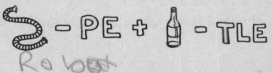

Robot
_ _ _ _ _

Answer: JACKIE RODOWSKY
ROBOT

13

MATCH UP

#1

Match up the clues in Column I with the answers in Column II and write the letters in the blanks on the opposite page.

I

1. The first to baby-sit for the Addisons
2. Mary Anne thinks she might want to be this when she grows up
3. Stacey's former best friend
4. Kristy and Bart both like this food
5. The Pikes' baby hamster
6. Watson's cat
7. Dawn is the only Baby-sitter who likes this pizza topping
8. Claudia's rag doll with yarn braids
9. Dawn's grandfather's occupation
10. She cheated from Claudia on a math test

II

a. Frodo
b. Anchovies
c. Teacher
d. Dawn
e. Banker
f. Laine
g. Boo-Boo
h. Shawna
i. Green peppers
j. Lennie

1. ____
2. ____
3. ____
4. ____
5. ____
6. ____
7. ____
8. ____
9. ____
10. ____

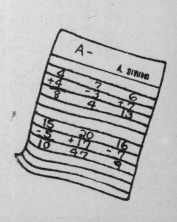

15

Word Jumble

BOYS BOYS BOYS

How much do you know about the Stoneybrook boys? This puzzle has three parts, and asks questions about dates, crushes, and kisses!

First answer the trivia questions.

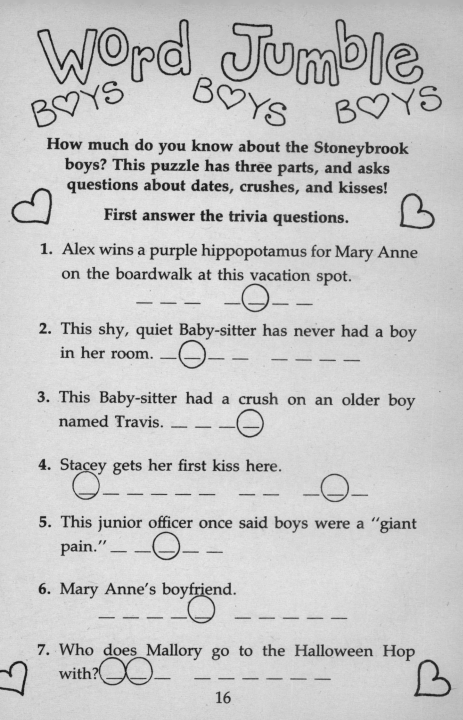

1. Alex wins a purple hippopotamus for Mary Anne on the boardwalk at this vacation spot.
   _ _ _   _(_)_ _

2. This shy, quiet Baby-sitter has never had a boy in her room. _(_)_ _   _ _ _ _ _

3. This Baby-sitter had a crush on an older boy named Travis. _ _ _(_)

4. Stacey gets her first kiss here.
   (_)_ _ _ _ _   _ _   _(_)_

5. This junior officer once said boys were a "giant pain." _ _(_)_ _

6. Mary Anne's boyfriend.
   _ _ _ _(_)   _ _ _ _ _

7. Who does Mallory go to the Halloween Hop with? (_)(_)_   _ _ _ _ _ _ _

16

8. Stacey goes out with this boy in Sea City.

_ _ _〇

9. Kristy has a huge crush on this boy.

_ _ _〇 _ _ _〇_ _

10. Mary Anne thinks Logan looks just like this movie star. _ _ _ _(_)_ _ _

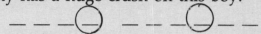

**Now unscramble the circled letters in your answers
to find the answer to the
SUPER TRIVIA QUESTION below.**

Example:

F R(I)E N D(S)
S(T)O N E(Y)(B)R O O K   I S T Y B B A
(B)(A)B I E S   Answer: BABY-SIT

**The circled letters in questions 1-5 are the letters in
the first part of the answer. Write them here.**

**The circled letters in questions 6-10 are the letters
in the second part of the answer. Write them here.**

SUPER TRIVIA QUESTION

**What is the name of the boy Claudia goes with to
the Final Fling?**

_ _ _ _ _ _   _ _ _ _ _ _

17

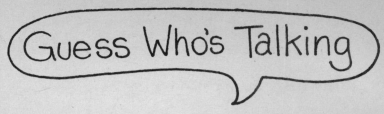

Guess Who's Talking

Everyone has their own personality, especially the members of the Baby-sitters Club. Can you identify which Baby-sitter is speaking from the quotes below?

1. "Mom gives me cab fare anytime I'm going more than ten feet away from the apartment, unless I'm going to be with a group of people."

2. "I'm not a good student, and I don't care about history or geography or science."

3. "In terms of looks, Logan is perfect."

4. "Karen usually leaves the rest of us in shock with her talk and excitement and enthusiasm."

5. "When I was two, my mom entered my picture in a baby contest and I won."

6. "Jessi and I were nervous wrecks waiting for the next meeting of the Baby-sitters Club."

7. "On the day of tryouts, all I had cared about was not doing something stupid."

Backwords Scramble
#2

The answer is SMITHTOWN, but what is the question? Unscramble the letters in the words below to solve this puzzle.

THAW SI HET MENA

FO EHT

ESRTRODE NOLCOILA

GLIVLAE REAN EAS TCYI?

___ ___ ___ ___   ___ ___   ___ ___ ___

___ ___ ___ ___   ___ ___

___ ___ ___

___ ___ ___ ___ ___ ___ ___ ___

___ ___ ___ ___ ___ ___ ___ ___

___ ___ ___ ___ ___ ___ ___

___ ___ ___ ___

___ ___ ___ ___ ___ ___ ___ ___ ?

Wördseărch
The members

Kristy, Claudia, Mary Anne, Stacey, Dawn, Jessi, and Mallory. Best friends forever! This three-part puzzle asks questions only about the members of the BSC.

First answer the questions.

1. Which club member has always lived on Bradford Court? _____

2. This member is originally from New York City. _____

3. Dawn's middle name. _____

4. Jessi helps Jackie Rodowsky build this for a science project. _____

5. Kristy's favorite professional sport. _____

6. This BSC member burns easily at the beach. _____

7. Claudia's bedroom walls are covered with her _____ -work.

8. Which Baby-sitter has two pierced holes in each ear? _____

9. Stacey's favorite movie. _____

10. Mary Anne's favorite movie star. _____

20

Now find all the answers in this word search. They are hidden horizontally, diagonally, vertically, and backward.

```
C  L  Y  R  A  E  G  M  A  C  V
A  U  D  C  I  A  K  L  R  I  O
S  T  Y  M  L  A  L  R  Y  A  L
N  M  Y  E  C  A  T  S  N  E  C
J  A  E  S  B  S  U  I  M  A  A
L  R  L  E  O  R  Y  D  D  A  N
W  Y  S  N  K  R  I  S  I  T  O
Y  A  D  J  E  S  S  R  E  A  D
B  N  I  A  R  T  C  L  A  U  D
I  N  A  M  W  A  L  L  O  R  Y
J  E  E  S  S  N  I  C  L  A  U
M  A  R  Y  P  O  P  P  I  N  S
D  I  A  M  A  L  L  O  R  Y  D
A  W  N  K  R  I  S  T  Y  M  A
R  Y  A  N  N  E  J  E  S  S  I
```

When you've circled the words in the puzzle, the remaining letters will spell out—from left to right —the names of all the BSC members except one. Her name is the answer to the super trivia question.

SUPER TRIVIA QUESTION

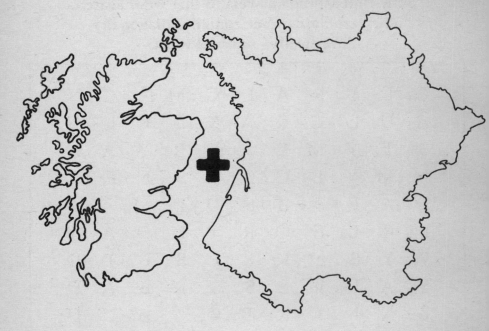

Which BSC member is of Scottish and French ancestry?

_____

Picture Puzzle

#2

To solve this puzzle, write the name of each picture in the blanks below. Cross out or add the indicated letters as you go along.

What is the name of Stacey's favorite New York City store?

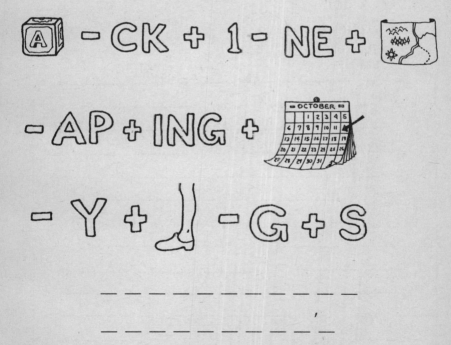

– CK + 1 – NE +

– AP + ING +

– Y +   – G + S

_ _ _ _ _ _ _ _ _ _ _

_ _ _ _ _ _ _ _ _ _

Answer:

23

MAZE
BATTER UP

Help! Kristy's Krushers have a softball game today and Kristy can't find her favorite baseball cap and glove. Can you lead the way?

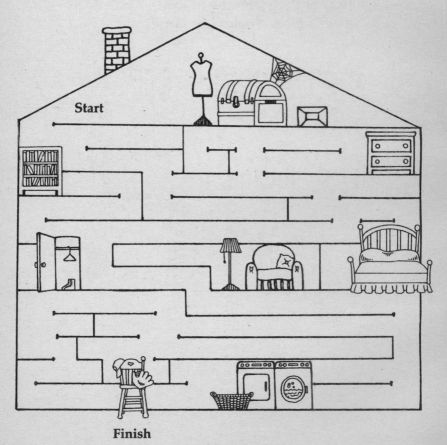

Start

Finish

Guess Who's Talking, Too!

Can you identify which BSC member is speaking from the quotes below?

1. "I have this weird thing sometimes, where even though I'm thrilled to get the lead, I kind of feel bad about it, too."

2. "I reached for the small silver-wrapped box and unwrapped it. When I lifted the lid I saw . . . a bracelet made of tiny gold hearts linked together."

3. "If I had to describe the ideal boy, it would be Travis. Tall, good-looking, with a fantastic smile and a great personality."

4. "Jessi and I are junior officers. To be honest, we don't have jobs. 'Junior officer' simply means that since we're eleven we're only allowed to sit during the daytime."

5. "I've always wanted a little brother or sister, and having Charlotte around for an entire week would be so much fun."

6. "My best friend in the whole world is Stacey McGill."

7. "I adore being in charge. Club meetings are the best times of my week."

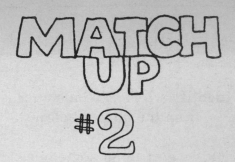

MATCH UP
#2

Match up the clues in Column I with the answers in Column II and write the letters in the blanks on the opposite page.

I

1. Leads the séance in Stacey's new house
2. Karen's "hotel game"
3. Sea City Restaurant
4. Claudia plays this outdoor game with the Rodowskys
5. Lost a tooth in a piece of candy
6. Dawn plays this finger game with Marnie
7. Stacey's first Broadway play
8. This substitute teacher accuses Claudia of cheating
9. She has the neatest handwriting in the BSC
10. Stacey's math teacher

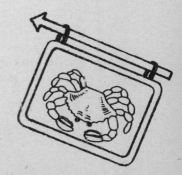

II

a. "Red Light, Green Light"
b. *Annie*
c. Mr. Zizmore
d. Vanessa
e. Mr. Zorzi
f. "Let's All Come In"
g. Mary Anne
h. Crabs for Grabs
i. Kristy
j. "Where Is Thumbkin?"

1. ___
2. ___
3. ___
4. ___
5. ___
6. ___
7. ___
8. ___
9. ___
10. ___

SCRAMBLE

Bring on the B📚📚ks

The BSC members love to read—just like you and your friends! Unscramble the ten titles below to find out which book your favorite Baby-sitter is most likely to curl up with.

Claudia has read this Newbery book:
H A R S A ,   I L P A N   N A D   L A T L

Jessi's favorite horse story:
S M P O I S I L B E   E H A C R L I

This is Dawn's favorite collection of ghost stories:
T I R I S P S ,   P O S O K S ,   D A N
H O S G T L Y   A L E T S

Mary Anne has read this classic three times:
N R U T H W E I G   G E H I H S T

Mallory's favorite horse story:
A AGOMRN ORF ANEMLID

Stacey and Charlotte have read this book together:
HET WROBROERS

Claudia has read this Nancy Drew mystery:
ETH TYMSREY FO TEH RVOIY
MCAHR

Jessi and Jamie have read this story about a ghost together:
GIREGOE'S WALHOELEN

Stacey gives this book to Charlotte:
HET KIRCTEC NI MIETS
RAUEQS

Mallory has read this book by Cynthia Voigt:
YEDCI'S NGSO

Word Jumble
WHO'S WHO

How many characters do you know in the Baby-sitters Club books? The answers to the questions in this puzzle are all names of people the club members know.

First answer the questions.

1. Who is Stacey baby-sitting for when a blackout occurs?

   _ _ (_) _ _ _ _ _ _   Johanssen

2. What is Kristy's mother's new married name?

   Mrs. _ _ _ _ _ (_)

3. Kristy's talkative stepsister.

   (_) _ _ _ _

4. Which Stoneybrook family has no children but *lots* of pets?

   The _ _ (_) _ _ _ _   family

5. Stacey's ex-best friend from New York City.

   _ _ _ _ (_)   Cummings

6. What is the name of the Stoneybrook Middle School principal?

   Mr. _ _ _ _ _ (_)

30

7. Jessi's little sister's nickname.

8. Claudia's brainy sister.

— — — — —⊖

9. This child is prone to car sickness.

— —⊖— —

10. Dawn's best friend from California.

Sunny⊖— — — — — —

Now unscramble the circled letters in your answers
to find the answer to the
SUPER TRIVIA QUESTION below.

**The circled letters in questions 1-5 are the letters in
the first part of the answer. Write them here.**

**The circled letters in questions 6-10 are the letters
in the second part of the answer. Write them here.**

SUPER TRIVIA QUESTION

**This child has to be escorted out of the haunted
house at Sudsy's Carnival because she is
frightened. Who is she?**

— — — — —   — — — — — —

THE NUMBERS GAME

1234 12345678910 123456

How Many?

7+6-1

2+2=4

5-

How's your memory? How about your math? The answers to the questions in this puzzle are all numbers.

5-3+2

First answer the questions.

3+2

1. How many times per week does the Baby-sitters Club meet? ☐

2. How many brothers and sisters does Mallory have? ☐

3. How many minutes long would three Baby-sitters club meetings be? ☐

4. How many junior officers are in the BSC? ☐

5. How many people (not including Aunt Cecelia) are in Jessi's family? ☐

Next add together the numbers in the boxes above, and write the answer here: ☐

5-3+2   2+2=4   6-1   subtract 17: −17

☐

7+6-1   7+   4   and divide by 3: ÷ 3

= ☐

32

Now you have the answer to the
SUPER TRIVIA QUESTION below.

SUPER TRIVIA QUESTION

2+2=4

According to Stacey, the Washington Mall is about _____ minutes away from Stoneybrook.

Backwords Scramble
#3

The answer is BUDDY BARRETT, but what is the question? Unscramble the letters in the sentence below to solve this puzzle.

HWO SHA A HURCS NO

COSASITEA SBC

EMBERM, ONHSANN OBLKIUENR?

_ _ _   _ _ _   _   _ _ _ _ _   _ _

_ _ _ _ _ _ _ _ _   _ _ _

_ _ _ _ _ _ ,   _ _ _ _ _ _ _

_ _ _ _ _ _ _ _ _ ?

Picture Puzzle

#3

To solve this puzzle, write the name of each picture in the blanks below. Cross out or add the indicated letters as you go along.

Which trendy restaurant do the Baby-sitters like to go to in New York City?

_ _ _ _ _ _ _

_ _ _ _

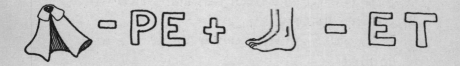

_ _ _ _ _ _ _

Answer:

CROSS WORD

ACROSS

4. Kristy can't stand this green vegetable
6. This BSC member would like to be an author
8. Dawn won't eat it (two words)
10. This Stoneybrook teenager has an IQ of 196
11. This club member is the shortest girl in the eighth grade
12. Stacey's favorite city (two words)
13. She has a secret passage in her bedroom
14. A BSC client who is a big practical joker

DOWN

1. She caught Dawn's mother's bouquet (two words)
2. Jessi is originally from this state (two words)
3. Dawn's hair color
5. How old was Dawn when she won a baby contest?
7. Kristy was born in this summer month
9. Mary Anne's office in the BSC

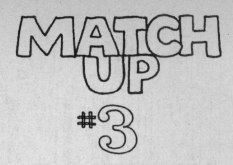

MATCH UP #3

Match up the clues in Column I with the answers in Column II and write the letters in the blanks on the opposite page.

I

1. Claudia likes to read this type of book
2. Mary Anne sneaks Tigger into the hospital to visit this friend
3. The third hole at Fred's Putt-Putt Course
4. Stacey's rose-scented perfume
5. Can peel a banana with her feet
6. Mallory wrote this story
7. Dances as Princess Aurora in the ballet, *Sleeping Beauty*
8. Mr. Pike makes this casserole with hot dog chunks in it
9. Discovers the old Hennessey house isn't really haunted
10. Kristy orders this at the Hard Rock Cafe

II

a. "Rainy Days and Froggy Nights"
b. Margo
c. Daddy Stew
d. Stacey
e. Mystery
f. "Old King Cole Hole"
g. Filet mignon
h. Jessi
i. Moonlight Mist
j. Claudia

1. ____
2. ____
3. ____
4. ____
5. ____
6. ____
7. ____
8. ____
9. ____
10. ____

Word Jumble
HIT OR MISS

Answer the trivia questions.

1. What is Claudia's club position?

   _ _ _(_)_ _ _ _ _ _ _ _(_)_ _

2. Stacey met this BSC member on the first day of school. _(_)_ _ _ _ _

3. Becca Ramsey fainted while playing a flower in this play.
   Little Red _ _ _ _ _ _ _ (_)_ _ _

4. What is Kristy's four-year-old stepbrother's name? _ _ _ _ _(_)

5. The Candy Kitchen in Sea City is famous for this treat.(_)_ _ _ _

6. Which club member has a sweat shirt that says "I'd rather be writing my novel?"

   _ _ _ _(_)_ _

7. Kristy's Krushers often practice at Stoneybrook Elementary on these days.

   (_)_ _ _ _ _ _ and Saturday

8. What is the name of the big city that is closest to Stoneybrook? _ _ _ _(_)(_)_ _

9. What kind of necklace does Mary Anne's dad give her on the day he marries Dawn's mother?

— (__) — (__) —

10. This relative moves in with Jessi's family to help out when Mrs. Ramsey goes back to work.

— (__)(__) — — — — — — — —

Now unscramble the circled letters in your answers to find the answer to the SUPER TRIVIA QUESTION below.

The circled letters in questions 1-4 are the letters in the first word of the answer. Write them here.

The circled letters in questions 5 and 6 are the letters in the second word of the answer. Write them here.

The circled letters in questions 7-10 are the letters in the third word of the answer. Write them here.

SUPER TRIVIA QUESTION

Mimi gets hooked on this game show while recovering from her stroke.

— — — — —   — —   — — — — — — — —

Answer:

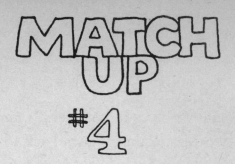

MATCH UP #4

**Match up the answers for Column I with Column
II and write them in the blanks
on the opposite page.**

I

1. Logan is originally from this state
2. Kristy dislikes this animal
3. Lives next-door to the Papadakises
4. Sunny Winslow lives in this state
5. "The Walking Disaster"
6. She dislikes the cold weather
7. Animal on Kristy's baseball cap
8. Stacey's ten-year-old doll
9. Has wire-rimmed glasses but hardly ever wears them
10. Penny sweetshop in Sea City

II

a. California
b. Jackie Rodowsky
c. Dog
d. Kentucky
e. Shannon
f. Mary Anne
g. Candy Heaven
h. Squirrel
i. Dawn
j. Amelia Jane

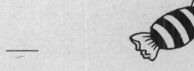

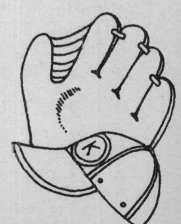

1. ____
2. ____
3. ____
4. ____
5. ____
6. ____
7. ____
8. ____
9. ____
10. ____

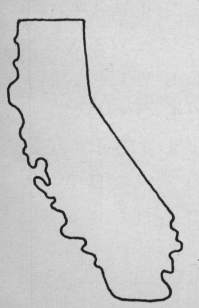

Wördsearch
THE NEIGHBORHOOD

Do you know your way around Stoneybrook? The ten Stoneybrook street names listed on the opposite page are hidden in the word search below. Can you find them? They are hidden horizontally, vertically, diagonally and backward.

```
S R N I E L L I V K C O R F Y Q U
E Q T H D C F P Z R L K E J N M B
D D L B J S A B Q G S O X I E S U
G R F O R L K I M B A L L E T B R
E J E R N A M F B A T P R H A C N
R C L C E N D G P Z E U A W L X T
S M Z K M I I F A W C E T T S I H
T E I U D G L H O F C E O Y E D I
O W D K O V J L S R V T R Q T F L
U S I B L Y I L Y E D R E E H V L
N P Y E L L A V Y R R E H C B U K
E W U K G M O O H V Y J C R B O A
```

Claudia lives on **Bradford** Court

Dawn and Mary Anne live on **Burnt Hill** Road

The Rodowskys live on **Reilly** Lane

Stacey once lived on **Fawcett** Avenue

The Barretts live on **Slate** Street

The Sobaks live on **Cherry Valley** Road

Edgerstoune Drive and **Ober** Road are in Kristy's neighborhood

The Johanssens live on **Kimball** Street

Alan Gray lives on **Rockville** Court

MAZE

COME HOME KITTY

**Mary Anne's kitten, Tigger, is lost.
Can you help Mary Anne find him?**

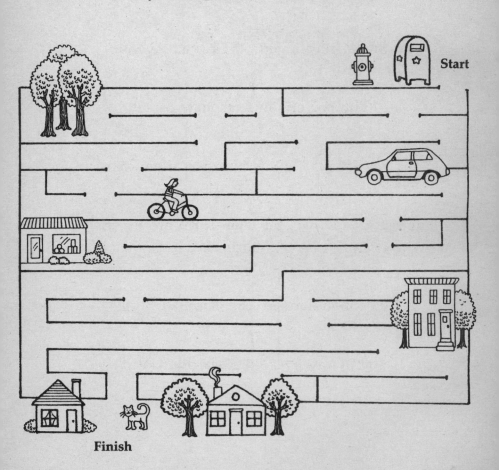

Start

Finish

Backwords Scramble
#4

The answer is FIRST GRADE, but what is the question? Unscramble the letters in the words below to solve this puzzle.

AHWT DRGAE EWRE

ETH STISABYTREB

NI NEWH A MRTSO TELF

OKBNYETSORO

HUITWOT ICTCELERTYI?

___ ___ ___   ___ ___ ___ ___ ___

___ ___ ___   ___ ___ ___

___ ___   - ___ ___ ___ ___ ___ ___ ___ ___

___ ___   ___ ___ ___ ___ ___

___ ___ ___ ___ ___ ___ ___ ___

___ ___ ___ ___ ___ ___ ___ ___

___ ___ ___ ___ ___ ___ ___ ___ ___ ?

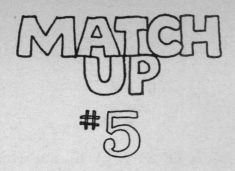

MATCH UP #5

**Match the answers for Column I with Column II
and write them in the blanks
on the opposite page.**

I

1. Her full name is Anastasia Elizabeth
2. Drinks one and a half cups of coffee every morning
3. Sudsy's Carnival is held here
4. Kristy's grandmother's old car
5. Toby's hometown
6. Claudia's love
7. She hates the color pink
8. Dawn's baby name
9. After being unemployed, Mr. Pike finds a job here
10. Stacey's best subject

II

a. Art
b. The Pink Clinker
c. Metro-Works
d. Mr. Spier
e. Math
f. Mary Anne
g. Carle Playground
h. Stacey
i. Lawrenceville
j. Sunshine

1. ____
2. ____
3. ____
4. ____
5. ____
6. ____
7. ____
8. ____
9. ____
10. ____

Picture Puzzle

#4

To solve this puzzle, write the name of each picture in the blanks below. Cross out or add the indicated letters as you go along.

What is the name of Dawn's favorite movie?

THE

__ __ __ __

 - E + ¢ - C

__ __ __ __ __ __ __ __

__ __ __ __

Answer:

ANSWERS

Page 8
Word Search: The Club

1. Wednesday, Friday
2. David Michael
3. Mallory
4. Monday
5. Kid-Kit
6. Agency
7. Five
8. Once
9. Kristy
10. Claudia

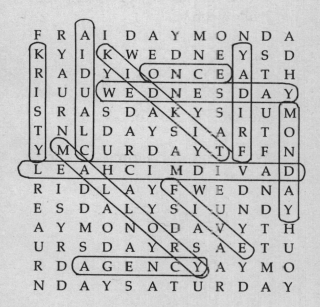

Super Trivia Question Answer:
Tuesday

Page 12
Backwards Scramble #1

Question:
WHAT IS THE NAME OF THE
TOY THAT IS STUCK IN
JACKIE RODOWSKY'S BATH-
ROOM DRAIN?

Answer: Blasto-Plane

Page 13
Picture Puzzle #1

Which charge did
Dawn help make a costume for
Halloween?

J A C K D I C E
R O A D T O W E L S K Y

Answer: Jackie Rodowsky

What kind of costume did they
make?

R O P E B O T T L E

Answer: Robot

Page 14
Match Up #1

1. d	5. a	9. e
2. c	6. g	10. h
3. f	7. i	
4. b	8. j	

Page 16
Word Jumble: Boys Boys Boys

1. Sea City
2. Mary Anne
3. Dawn
4. Tunnel of Luv
5. Jessi
6. Logan Bruno
7. Ben Hobart
8. Toby
9. Bart Taylor
10. Cam Geary

Super Trivia Question Answer:
Austin Bentley

Page 18
Guess Who's Talking

1. Stacey
2. Claudia
3. Mary Anne
4. Kristy
5. Dawn
6. Mallory
7. Jessi

Page 19
Backwards Scramble #2

Question:
WHAT IS THE NAME
OF THE RESTORED
COLONIAL VILLAGE NEAR
SEA CITY?

Answer: Smithtown

Page 20
Word Search: The Members

1. Claudia
2. Stacey
3. Read
4. Volcano
5. Baseball
6. Mary Anne
7. Art
8. Dawn
9. "Mary Poppins"
10. Cam Geary

```
C  L  Y  R  A  E  G  M  A  C  V
A  U  D  C  I  A  K  L  R  I  O
S  T  Y  M  L  A  L  R  Y  A  L
N  M  Y  E  C  A  T  S  N  E  C
J  A  E  S  B  S  U  I  M  A  A
L  R  L  E  O  R  Y  D  D  A  N
W  Y  S  N  K  R  I  S  I  T  O
Y  A  D  I  E  S  S  R  E  A  D
B  N  I  A  R  T  C  L  A  U  D
I  N  A  M  W  A  L  L  O  R  Y
J  E  E  S  S  N  I  C  L  A  U
M  A  R  Y  P  O  P  P  I  N  S
D  I  A  M  A  L  L  O  R  Y  D
A  W  N  K  R  I  S  T  Y  M  A
R  Y  A  N  N  E  J  E  S  S  I
```

Super Trivia Question Answer:

Stacey

Page 23
Picture Puzzle #2

What is Stacey's favorite New York City store?

B L O C K O N E M A P I N G D A Y L E G'S

Answer: Bloomingdale's

Page 24
Maze: Batter Up

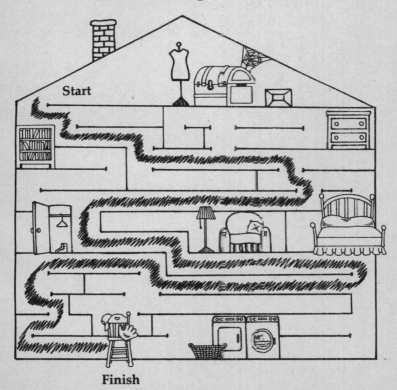

Start

Finish

Page 25
Guess Who's Talking, Too!

1. Jessi
2. Mary Anne
3. Dawn
4. Mallory
5. Stacey
6. Claudia
7. Kristy

Page 26
Match Up #2

1. i
2. f
3. h
4. a
5. d
6. j
7. b
8. e
9. g
10. c

Page 28
Scramble: Bring on the Books

Sarah, Plain and Tall
Impossible Charlie
Spirits, Spooks, and Ghostly Tales
Wuthering Heights
A Morgan for Melinda
The Borrowers
The Mystery of the Ivory Charm
Georgie's Halloween
The Cricket in Times Square
Dicey's Song

Page 30
Word Jumble: Who's Who

1. Charlotte
2. Brewer
3. Karen
4. Mancusi
5. Laine
6. Taylor
7. Becca
8. Janine
9. Margo
10. Winslow

Super Trivia Question Answer:
Karen Brewer

Page 32
The Numbers Game: How Many?

1.   3
2.   7
3.   90
4.   2
5.   5
     107
    −17
      90   divided by 3 = 30

Super Trivia Question Answer:
30 minutes

Page 34
Backwards Scramble #3

Question:
WHO HAS A CRUSH
ON ASSOCIATE
BSC MEMBER,
SHANNON KILBOURNE?

Answer: Buddy Barrett

Page 35
Picture Puzzle #3

Which trendy restaurant do the
Baby-sitters like to go to in
New York City?

H A T R Ø A D R O C K
C A P E F E E T

Answer: Hard Rock Cafe

Page 36
Crossword

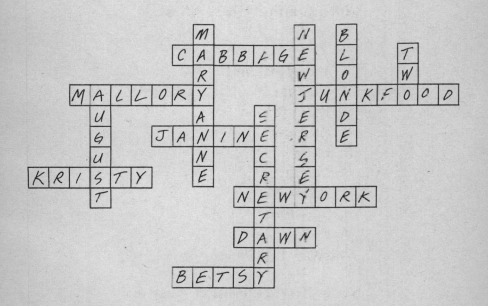

Page 38
Match Up #3

1. e
2. j
3. f
4. i
5. b
6. a
7. h
8. c
9. d
10. g

Page 40
Word Jumble: Hit or Miss

1. Vice-president
2. Claudia
3. Riding Hood
4. Andrew
5. Fudge
6. Mallory
7. Tuesday
8. Stamford
9. Pearl
10. Aunt Cecelia

Super Trivia Question Answer:
Wheel of Fortune

Page 42
Match Up #4

1. d
2. h
3. e
4. a
5. b
6. i
7. c
8. j
9. f
10. g

Page 44
Word Search: The Neighborhood

Page 46
Come home, Kitty!

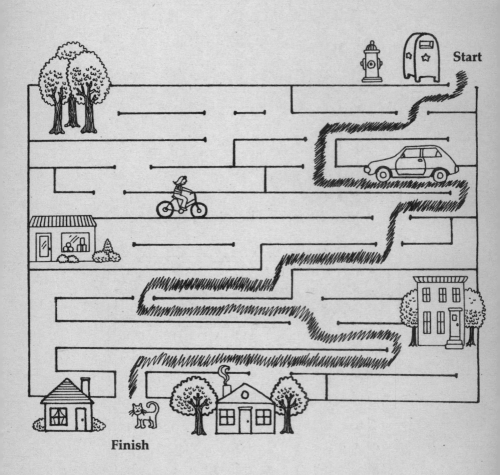

Start

Finish

Page 47
Backwards Scramble #4

Question:
WHAT GRADE WERE
THE BABY-SITTERS IN
WHEN A STORM LEFT
STONEYBROOK WITHOUT
ELECTRICITY?

Answer: First grade

Page 48
Match Up #5

1. h
2. d
3. g
4. b
5. i
6. a
7. f
8. j
9. c
10. e

Picture Puzzle #4

What is the name of Dawn's favorite movie?

<u>T H E</u> <u>P E A R C E N T</u>
<u>T R A P</u>

Answer: The Parent Trap